DEALING WITH
**MENTAL
DISORDERS**

DEALING WITH

# EATING
# DISORDERS

By Bethany Bryan

ReferencePoint
Press®

San Diego, CA

For more information, contact:
ReferencePoint Press, Inc.
PO Box 27779
San Diego, CA 92198
www.ReferencePointPress.com

Content Consultant: Carla Marie Manly, PhD

LIBRARY OF CONGRESS CATALOGING-IN-PUBLICATION DATA

Names: Bryan, Bethany, author.
Title: Dealing with eating disorders / Bethany Bryan.
Description: San Diego : ReferencePoint Press, 2020. | Series: Dealing with mental disorders | Includes bibliographical references and index. | Audience: Grades 10-12.
Identifiers: LCCN 2019034018 (print) | LCCN 2019034019 (eBook) | ISBN 9781682827895 (hardcover) | ISBN 9781682827901 (eBook)
Subjects: LCSH: Eating disorders--Juvenile literature. | Eating disorders--Treatment--Juvenile literature.
Classification: LCC RC552.E18 B7694 2020  (print) | LCC RC552.E18  (eBook) | DDC 616.85/26--dc23
LC record available at https://lccn.loc.gov/2019034018
LC eBook record available at https://lccn.loc.gov/2019034019

# CONTENTS

**INTRODUCTION**
HEATHER'S STRUGGLE.................... 4

**CHAPTER ONE**
WHAT ARE EATING DISORDERS?......... 10

**CHAPTER TWO**
HOW ARE EATING
DISORDERS DIAGNOSED? ..................26

**CHAPTER THREE**
WHAT IS LIFE LIKE WITH
AN EATING DISORDER?.................... 42

**CHAPTER FOUR**
HOW ARE EATING
DISORDERS TREATED? ................... 56

SOURCE NOTES ............................. 70
FOR FURTHER RESEARCH .................. 74
INDEX ................................... 76
IMAGE CREDITS............................ 79
ABOUT THE AUTHOR........................ 80

# INTRODUCTION

# HEATHER'S STRUGGLE

Heather was sixteen years old, tall, and athletic. She was the go-to power server on her school's volleyball team. Like a lot of teenagers, she had some insecurities about her body. She worried that she was too tall for boys to like her, that her chest was underdeveloped, and that her thighs looked too big in her volleyball uniform. Heather had dealt with these insecurities for a long time. When she was twelve, she attended a family reunion. Her Aunt Stacy made a comment that she should limit herself to just a few cookies from the dessert table because she was "looking a little chubby." Heather internalized the comment, and it negatively affected her self-image.

These types of comments can often have negative effects. Jen Gunter, a gynecologist who writes for the *New York Times*, recalled trying on an old dress of her mother's. She couldn't get it to zip. "'Hmmm,' my mother said. 'I guess you're too fat.' . . . I walked into that room a very tall and average-size girl. I walked out a fat girl."[1] As a result, Gunter has struggled with binge-eating disorder for forty years.

**Body image is how a person perceives her appearance. A negative body image can lead to unhealthy decisions.**

After the reunion, Heather did what a lot of girls her age do when they hear comments like her Aunt Stacy's. She went home and immediately put herself on a diet, eating half a grapefruit for breakfast, a cup of yogurt and a plain turkey burger for lunch, and a small bowl of vegetable soup for dinner. She began to experience hunger differently. Rather than listening to her body when her stomach growled, she started to brush the feeling aside. Hunger pangs began to feel like a victory over her uncontrollable "food demons." The hunger gave her a sense of control over her life for the first time. Heather started eating less and less, enjoying comments from people who said she looked good and made positive remarks about her weight loss. If she could just stick with it, Heather knew that she could be happy and live the kind of life she wanted.

But denying her normal food cravings caught up with her. Heather would have moments where she lost control. At a friend's birthday sleepover one weekend, she ate a second piece of pizza after telling herself she could have only one. To most people, two slices of pizza would be a normal meal. But for Heather, who was used to strict control of her diet, the second slice made her feel bad and guilty. However, she also felt strangely comforted by her pain, like it was a well-deserved punishment for losing control and eating more than she should have.

Heather became accustomed to the cycle of seeking comfort from food, followed by a period of punishing self-hatred. When she was feeling bad, afraid, stressed, or insecure, she would sneak food, like a carton of ice cream, back into her bedroom and finish it, even after she was full and feeling sick. After every binge, she would hide the evidence in her backpack and throw it out on her way to school the next day. Heather began feeling anxious every time she had to eat in front of others. Heather was not alone in this behavior.

"The first time I binged I was seven," said Sara-Romeo White in a 2015 article for BuzzFeed News. "And for a brief moment nothing else mattered.

**Exercise is important to be healthy, but overexercising can be dangerous. The body needs time to rest and recover.**

It made me numb and full and empty and outside of myself all at the same time."[2]

After every binge, Heather promised herself that it was the last one. She would start counting calories again the next morning or head out for a quick run before breakfast. For the next several weeks, she would feel in control again. But another binge was never far away. This cycle started to become a habit for Heather—a binge followed by sometimes very extreme changes to her diet and a compulsion to exercise until it hurt. Often, exercise addiction goes hand-in-hand with disordered eating patterns. Many people who struggle with eating disorders find that they are compelled to exercise. This could be in preparation for calories they will consume, to burn off a meal, or even to punish themselves for having eaten.

**People who suffer from eating disorders often have other mental health concerns, such as depression or anxiety. These are called co-occurring disorders.**

Tara Fuller struggles with exercise addiction. She recalled the effect it had on her daily life: "I was getting insanely tired, but I fought through it by drinking tons of coffee and cutting back on other activities."[3]

Heather is suffering from binge-eating disorder, a mental disorder characterized by feelings of losing control and overeating. Sufferers of binge-eating disorder feel a sense of shame when it comes to eating. They might eat when not physically hungry or eat more rapidly than usual. After a binge, they might feel depressed, anxious, isolated, and hopeless. Then the cycle will start all over again.

Binge-eating disorder is one of several kinds of eating disorders. In a general sense, an eating disorder is a type of mental condition characterized by a pattern of eating and sometimes exercise behaviors that are abnormal and obsessive. These behaviors can ultimately have an effect on a person's health. Many who suffer from an eating disorder engage in starvation habits or bingeing and purging. This can result in malnutrition, low body weight, or an inability to regulate body temperature. Some people might become very thin. But others don't show any outward sign of having an eating disorder. Like Heather, many with binge-eating disorder have an average weight or are overweight. "I have always lived in a higher weight body," said Chevese Turner, the founder of the Binge-Eating Disorder Association, who has struggled with both anorexia and binge-eating disorder in the past.

Eating disorders have been around for centuries. But the late twentieth century brought a change. Mental health professionals began to extensively study eating disorders for the first time, working to help those who suffer from them get on a path to recovery. Eating disorders are complicated, are often tied into other mental health concerns, and can be life-threatening. This is why it's important to understand how and why an eating disorder can develop, how to recognize one, where to go for help, and ways to navigate the path to recovery. Longtime eating disorder sufferer Kimberly Neil wrote an article in *Teen Vogue* about her own path to recovery. She said, "Having an eating disorder is never a choice. . . . Healing takes nonstop effort and requires so much support, but it is possible."[4]

"Healing takes nonstop effort and requires so much support, but it is possible."[4]

*– Kimberly Neil, on her eating disorder recovery*

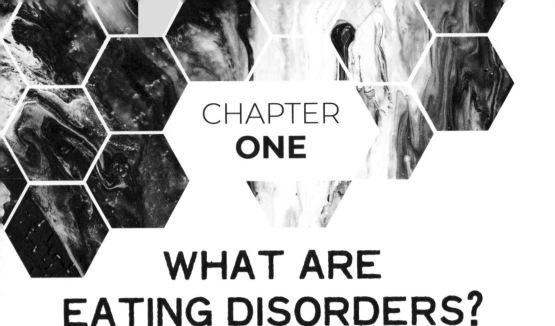

# CHAPTER
## ONE

# WHAT ARE
# EATING DISORDERS?

At least 30 million Americans suffer from an eating disorder in their lifetime, according to the National Association of Anorexia Nervosa and Associated Disorders (ANAD). Eating disorders have a high mortality rate compared with other mental disorders. So, what are they? Eating disorders are mental disorders that affect people's relationship with and behaviors around food and fitness. These disorders also affect the value people place on themselves through body image. In the past, eating disorders have been associated with young women, but these conditions can affect anyone at any age.

## ANOREXIA NERVOSA

Anorexia nervosa is a pattern of behaviors that results in self-starvation. People with anorexia associate their self-worth with thinness. Essentially, they feel that if they're thin, they're good; if they gain weight, they're bad. Therefore, they go to great lengths to prevent weight gain. Some carefully monitor their calorie intake. They might take laxatives or diuretics, medications that cause them to use the bathroom more often. In their

**Many people think only women have eating disorders. This can make it harder for men to be diagnosed and receive help.**

minds, waste creates extra weight in the body and they need to get rid of it as soon as possible. They might vomit to rid themselves of any food they've ingested, or they might engage in fasting. Some anorexics exercise obsessively, sometimes several times a day. They might weigh themselves frequently and carefully monitor the results. Eating becomes a source of stress. Not eating eventually becomes an obsession, and people plan their days around it. Anorexia is often tied to other mental disorders like depression, anxiety, obsessive-compulsive disorder, or substance abuse. It shares certain behaviors with those conditions. Many experts believe that eating disorders like anorexia give sufferers a sense of control over some aspect of their lives when they feel they have lost

## LORD BYRON'S DIET

Poet Lord Byron (1788–1824) is sometimes considered the father of fad diets, in one of his lesser-known accomplishments. Byron believed himself to have a "morbid propensity to fatten," and therefore maintained a strict diet of biscuits, soda water, and potatoes soaked in vinegar. He often wore warm clothing to force his body to sweat off the excess weight. Other times, he would eat a large meal and then take magnesia, a laxative. Byron kept close tabs on his weight, recording that he weighed 194 pounds (88 kg) in 1806. By 1811, he weighed only 126 pounds (57 kg). By 1816, Byron's diet consisted of a thin slice of bread and some tea for breakfast, and vegetables and seltzer water for dinner. In the evenings, he might have a cup of green tea. Experts like Arthur Crisp, a professor of psychiatric medicine at St. George's Hospital in London, believe that Byron's behaviors were probably the result of anorexia nervosa.

*Quoted in Louise Foxcroft, "Lord Byron: The Celebrity Diet Icon," BBC News, January 3, 2012. http://bbcnews.com.*

control in other ways. According to Emily Troscianko, who battled anorexia in the past, "The sufferer attempts to take control of her life by exerting control over one section of her life, her diet and thereby her body, and illness develops when that exertion of control turns into its opposite, the state of being controlled by a pathological compulsion to control."[5]

Eventually, these behaviors will begin to manifest themselves physically. A person with anorexia will often appear very thin. But this isn't always the case. Many who suffer from anorexia hide their bodies under larger clothing to keep signs of extreme weight loss a secret. Some may hide these symptoms so well, they don't appear to be sick at all. Beyond outward appearance, an anorexia sufferer might be tired all the time or suffer from insomnia. A person with anorexia will often have a low tolerance for cold weather. In extreme cases, female anorexics will stop having a period. An anorexic's hair might begin to thin and fall out. The body begins to break down muscle for fuel when not fed properly. The heart is a muscle. Because of this, people with anorexia might start to have heart problems, like low blood pressure or irregular rhythms. Anorexia can even lead to heart failure. People with anorexia

often develop a fine coating of hair on the arms and legs, called lanugo. Lanugo is the body's way of trying to protect itself from the heat loss associated with extreme thinness.

In some cases, patients have died from anorexia. Two famous cases of this are musician Karen Carpenter and French model Isabelle Caro. Caro participated in an anorexia awareness ad campaign in 2007. She was featured on billboards, posing in the nude to show the devastating effects of her disease. The billboards said "No Anorexia" in Italian. "The idea was to shock people into awareness," Caro said. "I decided to do it to warn girls about the danger of diets and of fashion commandments."[6] Caro passed away in 2010. Death is often the result of heart failure, but one in five anorexia deaths are due to suicide. In addition to links to other mental disorders, such as depression, anorexia can affect a person's mood and emotional well-being.

## BULIMIA NERVOSA

Bulimia differs from anorexia in several key ways. People with bulimia have recurrent episodes of binge eating. They eat more food than would be considered normal, and they feel a lack of control. But before the body can fully absorb nutrients from food, bulimics purge it through self-induced vomiting, laxatives, enemas, or other means. As with anorexia, those with bulimia do not have a healthy relationship with food. They can be plagued by weight and body self-evaluation issues.

People who suffer from bulimia may deal with low self-esteem, and they often struggle to maintain relationships with others. They might also deal with anxiety, depression, bipolar disorder, a personality disorder like borderline personality disorder (BPD), or substance abuse. Some of the physical symptoms of bulimia are not outwardly apparent. People with bulimia will often be dehydrated because of excessive purging. This can lead to eventual kidney problems. They sometimes deal with digestive issues from frequent vomiting or laxative abuse. Some struggle with tooth decay or severe gum disease from vomiting, since stomach acid can damage the teeth. As with anorexia, many female bulimics will miss periods or stop having a period altogether. They might also struggle with cardiovascular issues, such as an irregular heartbeat or heart failure. Bulimia is often connected to acts of self-harm, like cutting, burning, or

## AMY WINEHOUSE AND HER FIGHT WITH BULIMIA

Singer Amy Winehouse rose to stardom in 2006 with her second album, *Back to Black*. Her voice was strong and sultry. She wore a trademark beehive hairdo, winged eyeliner, and fun, flamboyant clothes. Unfortunately, her death in 2011 didn't surprise many of her friends and fans. It was common knowledge that Winehouse had struggled with heroin and alcohol addiction for years. In her trademark song, "Rebab," she even sang about resisting getting help for her addictions. But when people remember the singer, they often overlook the other thing that helped to take her life: bulimia nervosa. The 2015 documentary about her life, *Amy*, reveals that Winehouse struggled with bulimia starting in her mid-teens. In interviews, her brother Alex has said that he believes the eating disorder contributed to her death. In 2013 he said, "She would have died eventually, the way she was going, but what really killed her was the bulimia."

*Quoted in Greg Moskovitch, "Amy Winehouse's Brother Says, 'What Really Killed Her Was Bulimia,'" MusicFeeds, June 23, 2013. http://musicfeeds.com.au.*

**Low self-esteem is a large risk factor for eating disorders. People with eating disorders sometimes believe their worth is based on their appearance.**

hitting oneself without the intention of attempting suicide. People who suffer from bulimia can also struggle with suicidal thoughts or actions. Oscar-nominated actress Gabourey Sidibe published her memoir, *This Is Just My Face: Try Not to Stare*, in 2017. In it, she talks about suicidal thoughts she experienced during her own bout with bulimia: "I wasn't afraid to die, and if there was a button I could've pushed to erase my existence from earth, I would have pushed it because it would have been easier and less messy than offing myself."[7]

## BINGE-EATING DISORDER

Binge-eating disorder is similar to bulimia in that a sufferer might consume a large amount of food in a short period of time, but binge eaters don't engage in purging behaviors. Those who suffer from a binge-eating disorder feel like their eating is outside of their control, and they will eat more than is considered normal in a given period of time.

Binge-eating disorder was first analyzed in a 1959 paper written by psychiatrist Albert Stunkard. Stunkard was studying obesity and eating patterns. He noticed that some of his subjects were experiencing bingeing periods where they uncontrollably ate large amounts of food. He related this condition to bulimia. It wasn't until 2013 that the American Psychiatric Association (APA) finally declared binge-eating disorder to be a separate disorder from bulimia. Binge-eating disorder is the most common eating disorder in the United States. A 2007 study found that 3.5 percent of American women and 2 percent of American men struggle with the disorder in their lifetime.

The symptoms of binge-eating disorder are different from those endured by people with anorexia or bulimia. Binge eating may make the sufferer feel better in the moment, but the long-term effects include negative self-evaluation and negative mood. Binge-eating disorder is characterized by marked emotional distress and at least three bingeing behaviors. These include feeling disgusted, guilty, or depressed after eating, eating more quickly than normal, eating until uncomfortably full, eating large amounts of food when not hungry, and eating in isolation due to embarrassment. Binge eaters struggle to eat around others, and they often feel as if they must eat in secret. This can lead to isolation, difficulties maintaining friendships, or struggles at work. Negative mood is the most common trigger, but others include restraining food intake, body weight negativity, and negative feelings about food. Binge eating can often result in extreme weight gain. Some cases of obesity can lead to joint problems, heart disease, type 2 diabetes, digestive issues, or sleep apnea.

Singer and actress Janet Jackson spoke about her experiences with binge-eating disorder in a 2010 interview: "Food has always brought me comfort and the bingeing is triggered when I'm in a space that is not positive. . . . Afterwards I'll beat myself up about it. I regret doing it, but I'll turn around and do it again."[8]

## OTHER EATING DISORDERS AND BEHAVIORS

Doctors continue to learn more about eating disorders. They are recognizing new conditions and behaviors all the time. One common disorder that has only recently been linked to other eating disorders is pica. Pica is a condition in which sufferers develop cravings for and eat things not meant for consumption. They might eat feces, hair, cloth, rocks, dirt, laundry detergent, or other unsuitable material. Fifty-two-year-old Donna Lee habitually consumed baby powder for almost two decades. "It felt comforting when I did it. I would feel satisfied," she said.[9] Some people with pica struggle with an intellectual disability, a form of autism, or schizophrenia. Others crave certain things because of a nutritional deficiency or malnourishment. Pregnant women sometimes develop pica because of iron deficiency. Pica is a dangerous condition, as consuming nonfood items can result in intestinal blockages or damage to teeth or other parts of the digestive system.

Rumination syndrome is another eating disorder. With this condition, sufferers regurgitate food soon after eating and either reswallow it or spit

**People with ARFID are not necessarily looking to lose or control weight. However, they can develop health complications similar to anorexia.**

it out. This condition can result in unintentional weight loss and is often linked to anxiety, depression, or another mental disorder.

Avoidant/restrictive food intake disorder (ARFID) is a condition in which sufferers fail to meet their necessary nutritional and energy needs. People with ARFID might have a lack of interest in food, fear negative consequences of eating, or avoid food based on sensory characteristics. These might include certain colors, textures, or smells. ARFID results in significant weight loss, like anorexia. However, the lack of interest in eating is not due to fear of weight gain or negative body image. It's a fear of choking or another consequence of eating. People with ARFID often struggle to gain enough weight to be healthy. They also struggle with basic nutrition requirements.

## DISORDERED EATING

Finally, there are behaviors that are often associated with eating disorders, but the behaviors themselves are not diagnosed. This is called disordered eating. According to a 2008 survey conducted by *SELF* magazine, around 65 percent of American women between the ages of twenty-five and forty-five struggled with disordered eating. But disordered eating can affect people of any gender. Disordered eating is often associated with obsessive dieting, fear of weight gain, and negative body image. Disordered eaters might purge, engage in self-starvation, or binge eat. But they do not meet the severity or time period required for a formal eating disorder diagnosis. Many people don't even recognize that what they're doing is disordered. They just think they're on a normal path to maintaining good health through diet or exercise. They might not notice that they've already reached a normal weight. "Recognizing what's normal and what's dangerous is the first step all women can take in developing a more positive body image and a healthier approach to food," said *SELF* editor-in-chief Lucy Danzinger.[10]

There are some types of disordered eating that, while not officially listed in diagnostic manuals, are recognized by some experts in the field. The term *orthorexia* was coined in 1998. It describes an obsessive behavior toward healthy eating to the point where it begins to actually damage the body. People experiencing orthorexia avoid certain foods altogether, believing them to be impure or unhealthy. A health-conscious person might read that he should limit sugar intake. He might cut out the excess by avoiding soft drinks, alcohol, or certain processed snack foods. A person experiencing orthorexia may read the same information but decide to cut out all sugar, including fruits and certain vegetables that are actually healthy, out of fear of consuming any sugar at all.

> "Recognizing what's normal and what's dangerous is the first step all women can take in developing a more positive body image and a healthier approach to food."[10]
>
> – SELF editor-in-chief Lucy Danzinger

Diabulimia, or Eating Disorder Diabetes Mellitus Type 1 (ED-DMT1) is an eating disorder restricted to certain people with type 1 diabetes, a condition in which the body doesn't produce insulin. Insulin is the hormone that carries a sugar called glucose to the cells, giving the body the energy it needs to function. People with type 1 diabetes have to give themselves insulin, typically through an injection or automatic pump, in order to manage their blood sugar levels. People with ED-DMT1 will restrict the amount of insulin they give themselves in order to lose weight. They might restrict the types of food they eat in order to avoid having to use insulin. Those with ED-DMT1 will often struggle with elevated blood sugar, which can result in blindness, low circulation in the hands and feet, kidney problems, heart disease, or liver disease. Uncontrolled type 1 diabetes often leads to an early death, so this type of eating disorder is extremely dangerous.

## WHAT CAUSES EATING DISORDERS?

There is no one definitive cause of eating disorders, such as a virus or bacteria invading the body. Rather, doctors cite multiple potential causes, including genetics, specific personality traits, social factors, other underlying mental disorders, emotional problems, and past trauma.

Whether genetics is a specific cause of eating disorders is still under research. A study carried out at the University of California, San Diego, from 1996 to 2002 monitored approximately 2,000 patients who suffered from either anorexia nervosa or bulimia. The goal was to help determine the role of genetics in their conditions, particularly for patients who are prone to relapse. The study concluded that there isn't a single gene that makes patients develop an eating disorder. More likely, genetics contributes to personality traits that are linked to the likelihood of eating disorders. These personality traits differ for each disorder, but include things like impulsivity, shyness, tendency to worry, perfectionism, and novelty-seeking behaviors. Novelty-seeking behaviors involve seeking out new experiences that release dopamine and adrenaline into the body, giving people a natural high. Dopamine is the chemical the brain releases when a person experiences love. Genetics can also increase a person's likelihood to develop other mental disorders with links to eating disorders, like depression and anxiety. Cases of eating disorders also seem to run in families, which suggests that there might be a genetic cause. But many experts suggest that this could instead be the result of learned behaviors within families. Singer Demi Lovato spoke publicly about her past issues with bulimia in 2016. In an article for *SELF* magazine, clinical psychologist Alicia H. Clark said of Lovato, "It's possible Demi learned it from watching her mom, who learned it from watching her mom. Watching a parent engage in disordered-eating behavior is hugely impactful as girls struggle to maintain an unrealistic body shape when going through adolescence and developing curves."[11]

**Demi Lovato has been open about her struggles with mental health and bulimia. Lovato has become an advocate for body positivity.**

In some eating disorder cases, the root cause might involve past trauma or emotional issues. For many people, food is linked to emotional well-being. Some people eat when they're feeling stressed, overwhelmed, sad, or uncomfortable, because it makes them feel a bit better in the moment. Movies, books, or TV shows in which a person is going through a breakup often portray that character eating ice cream or candy. Food gives some people a sense of comfort because it releases dopamine in the brain. It's a kind of reward for a good feeling. When this type of eating gets out of control, it's called emotional eating. Sometimes it makes people feel as if they can't stop eating as they continue to chase the dopamine high.

Trauma and resulting disorders like post-traumatic stress disorder (PTSD) can also contribute to eating disorders. According to a 2011 study, approximately one-third of women with bulimia met the criteria for PTSD. Another 20 percent of women in the study had binge-eating disorder. "Purging can be seen as a way to get rid of something unwanted (emotion, memory, or symptom) while bingeing can be seen as a way to fill a void," said Dr. Carolyn Coker Ross, a doctor who specializes in treating eating disorders.[12]

> "Purging can be seen as a way to get rid of something unwanted (emotion, memory, or symptom) while bingeing can be seen as a way to fill a void."[12]
>
> – Dr. Carolyn Coker Ross

## THE ROLE OF THE DIET INDUSTRY

One of the biggest and most far-reaching factors that contributes to eating disorders is society's interest in dieting and weight loss. The word *diet* can be traced back to the ancient Greek word *diaita*. It was a term that described a person's complete lifestyle choices, including how they ate, how they drank, and how they exercised. The idea was to urge ancient Greeks to adopt the idea that a healthy body leads to a healthy mind. Early Christianity later equated gluttony with sin. Psychotherapist Dr. Sharon K. Farber explains, "In the middle ages, Christian saints and mystics, wanting to suffer like Jesus, starved and hurt themselves as they went into trances. Some, like Saint Catherine of Siena, were even canonized as saints."[13]

In the long term, this helped to shape the way that people view the relationship between food, weight, and self-worth. Many people continue to believe that being fat is bad and a sign of weakness, while thin bodies

# THE GROWTH OF THE
## DIET INDUSTRY

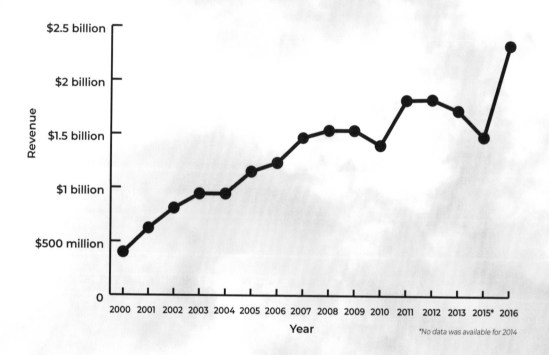

This graph shows the yearly revenues for diet and weight loss centers from 2000–2016.

*Sources: Gale Business Insights: Global, 2019; Gale Company Intelligence Database, 2019*

represent self-control, discipline, and inherent goodness. Dieting has long been the chosen way for people to achieve that thin ideal.

There are many different kinds of diets. In some, a person limits food intake and monitors calorie counts. In others, people might deprive themselves of certain foods, like foods containing sugar, or even limit themselves to specific types of food. The raw food diet consists of mostly fruits, nuts, vegetables, and seeds, with none to be heated above 118 degrees Fahrenheit (48 degrees C). The cabbage soup diet calls for almost nothing but cabbage soup for every meal.

This urge to diet is helped along by the diet industry, worth an estimated $169 billion in 2016. And this industry is expected to continue growing to an estimated worth of $279 billion by 2023. Dieting is often portrayed in the media as a way to fix people's bodies, and in doing so, fix their lives. People adopt this idea for themselves, motivated by others' stories of success on one diet or another. But the body has natural survival mechanisms that can make it hard to lose weight. When a person begins to lose weight quickly, the body's survival instincts kick in and the metabolism slows down to keep a person from starving to death. The human body feels like it's starving, so it fights back. Many people fall into eating disorders and disordered habits because they feel pressure to diet from society, a family member, a romantic partner, friends, a sports coach, or a number of other outside influences. When they struggle with the diet because the body doesn't want to starve, a negative cycle often begins. The person restricts food intake by dieting, the body craves food, a binge occurs, and the unhealthy cycle is set in motion. Often, the result is disordered eating or an eating disorder.

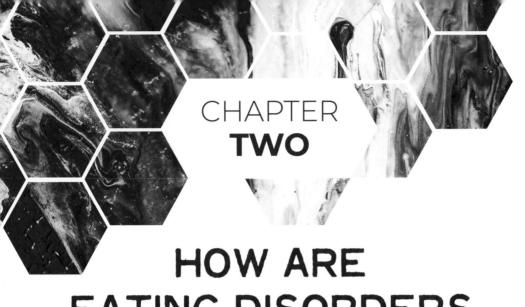

# HOW ARE
# EATING DISORDERS
# DIAGNOSED?

**H**istorical evidence suggests that eating disorders are nothing new. Descriptions of what were likely cases of anorexia nervosa date back to the twelfth and thirteenth centuries, when people believed that food was sin and starved themselves as a sign of devotion to God. Finally, English physician William Gull coined the term *anorexia nervosa* in 1873. At that point, eating disorders began to be treated like medical and mental conditions. A century later, in 1973, a pediatric psychiatrist named Hilde Bruch wrote a book called *Eating Disorders: Obesity, Anorexia Nervosa, and the Person Within*. This book was one of the first to relate food issues with human emotion. So, while eating disorders have been around for centuries, research is still relatively new. Doctors and mental health care providers are still learning what constitutes an eating disorder, how it affects the human body, and how to treat it effectively.

In the 1960s, thin was in. At the height of her fame, a world-famous model by the name of Lesley Hornby stood at 5.5 feet (1.7 m) and

**Twiggy helped pioneer women's fashion in the 1960s. After Twiggy, fashion designers began using thinner and thinner models.**

weighed 92 pounds (42 kg). Her trademark thin body earned her the nickname "Twiggy," and that is the name she still goes by today. Fashion often determines which body types are in vogue. Twiggy, with the help of fashion icon and first lady Jacqueline Kennedy, ushered in an era of drop waists and colorful shift dresses, miniskirts, voluminous hair, and dramatic makeup. These new styles pushed aside the idealized Marilyn Monroe hourglass shape that women strived for in the 1950s. Women in the 1960s and 1970s wanted to look like Twiggy. They wanted to look more androgynous than the hyperfeminized fifties had allowed them to be. They wanted short-cut wash-and-wear hairstyles; long, thin legs and arms; delicate, slender bodies; and big, dramatic doe eyes, thanks to layers upon layers of false eyelashes. Twiggy's thin body type quickly became the ideal, even though Twiggy herself never felt that confident. "I was this funny, skinny little thing with eyelashes and long legs, who had grown up hating how I looked," she said in a 2016 interview.[14]

> "I was this funny, skinny little thing with eyelashes and long legs, who had grown up hating how I looked."[14]
>
> – Model and actress Twiggy, on her own self-confidence at the height of her career

Despite how Twiggy felt about her body, a lot of women made terrible sacrifices to attain one just like it. Eating disorders were on the rise, but no one knew how to handle the problem just yet. Anorexia research was still in its infancy, and mental health professionals didn't quite understand how it connected to bingeing and purging behaviors.

In 1972, a woman checked herself into a hospital in London. She was treated by psychologist Gerald Russell. Russell was familiar with cases of anorexia, but this woman's symptoms were very different. This patient wasn't underweight or emaciated, but she was malnourished. There was something wrong, even if it wasn't anorexia.

This woman's disorder was one of the first recognized cases of bulimia. Russell wrote a paper in 1979, describing bulimia as its own

**Stereotypes about who can develop eating disorders can make it harder for people to recognize the problem or receive help. People of any race, gender, or age can develop an eating disorder.**

disorder: "The majority of the patients had a previous history of true or cryptic anorexia nervosa. Self-induced vomiting and purging are secondary devices used by the patients to counteract the effects of overeating and prevent a gain in weight."[15]

It was another eight years before bulimia was added to the *Diagnostic and Statistical Manual of Mental Disorders (DSM)*. The *DSM* is the authoritative guide used by mental health professionals to offer patients an official diagnosis of a mental disorder. As of 2019, the fifth edition of the *DSM (DSM-5)* is the most current. Bulimia received its own entry, apart from anorexia. This was an important moment for bulimia sufferers, because their disorder now had a name. It wasn't just a bad habit that someone could quit at a moment's notice. It required professional care and treatment, and that care could now be covered by a patient's insurance. The first step to treating an eating disorder became getting a diagnosis.

## WHO GETS EATING DISORDERS?

There's a popular myth that eating disorders are predominantly found in white girls and women. This is likely because white women dominated early diagnoses and famous cases. But anyone can struggle with an eating disorder.

Studies suggest that while men get eating disorders, they are simply more reluctant to seek help for a disorder that they might associate with femininity. However, according to the National Eating Disorders Association (NEDA), ten million men in the United States will experience an eating disorder in their lives. "No one realized I had a disorder," a contributor named Isaac said in a 2017 article for BuzzFeed, "and they didn't believe me when I told them. My sister thought I was doing it for attention and trying to be 'cool.'"[16]

> "No one realized I had a disorder, and they didn't believe me when I told them."[16]
>
> *– Isaac, who began to struggle with an eating disorder in seventh grade*

Eating disorders are also a struggle among transgender people. According to a survey of around 300,000 college students, transgender and nonbinary individuals are more than four times as likely as their cisgender peers to be diagnosed with anorexia or bulimia. They are two times more likely to experience disordered eating and related behaviors, such as purging, than their cisgender peers. Sixteen percent of the transgender students surveyed reported being diagnosed with an eating disorder. The survey was focused on self-reported eating disorders or eating disorder behaviors, such as purging or using laxatives. Transgender activist Luke Knudsen said, "My eating disorder allowed me to control the parts of me I was too scared to show the world, the parts that were too masculine to exist in a feminine body, the parts that were scared that my parents would find out they didn't have the perfect daughter they thought they had."[17]

The risks of eating disorders extend to all ethnic groups. Black teenagers are 50 percent more likely to experience bingeing and purging behaviors than white teenagers. Latinx people are more likely to struggle with bulimia than their non-Latinx peers. The study of eating disorders among Native Americans and Alaska Natives has long been neglected, but binge-eating disorders and other related issues are becoming more recognized among these communities. Doctors are often to blame for ignoring or dismissing eating disorders in nonwhite patients. This happened to author and eating disorder advocate Stephanie Covington Armstrong. "Everyone assumed all of the stereotypes: Black girls are more comfortable with our bodies. We like being heavier. We don't develop eating disorders. So I could hide in plain sight," she said.[18]

> "My eating disorder allowed me to control the parts of me I was too scared to show the world."[17]
>
> *– Luke Knudsen, on experiencing an eating disorder as a trans man*

Eating disorders can affect people of any age. For example, rumination syndrome is commonly found in infants and young children. At the other end, 13 percent of women over fifty experience behaviors related to eating disorders.

## SIGNS OF A PROBLEM

It can be difficult to detect and diagnose eating disorders. Since eating disorders are all about maintaining a kind of control over one's life, people struggling with an eating disorder are often reluctant to let go of that control. They might not want to admit that they have a problem. They might learn to hide their behaviors, wearing oversized clothing to cover up a significant weight loss or purging in private. Due to society's prizing of thinness, a person's weight loss might be seen as a good thing rather than a cause for alarm. Even if a friend or family member notices that something is wrong, a person who is struggling might deny that there's an issue. Finally, normalization of dieting and self-soothing through food, such as "bingeing on pizza" with friends, can make it difficult to recognize a problem. Kevin Watson has struggled with an eating disorder. He wrote online about hiding it from family and friends: "What most people in my life don't know is that after every meal, no matter how small, I am instantly nauseous. Most of the time I try to eat alone so people don't notice it[,] so they don't see how immensely painful and uncomfortable it is."[19]

Sometimes getting help requires an intervention by a doctor or loved one. Even then, a person has to accept the help and have a desire to change the behavior. In order to get an official diagnosis, a patient must meet certain specific diagnostic criteria outlined by the *DSM-5*.

There are certain behaviors tied into eating disorders that might be a sign that a person is struggling. Those who suffer from certain eating disorders are often so preoccupied with food, weight, and body image that they are led to chronic dieting. Some people might adopt an equal input and output strategy. This means only eating what can be exercised off later, even if that means fasting or going to the gym multiple times

**Society normalizes self-soothing with food, which can lead to difficulty identifying eating disorders. Learning other methods of self-soothing is often helpful in preventing and treating eating disorders.**

a day. Others feel they must restrict certain foods, such as anything containing carbohydrates or fats. Maintaining social habits around food often becomes a struggle. People might cook a huge meal for friends, only to eat none of it. They might feel stressed about going out to dinner or experience anxiety when asked to be spontaneous, especially about food. They might become withdrawn and isolated from friendships and family events. People suffering from an eating disorder might also live in fear of becoming fat, even after losing weight. They might find themselves scrutinizing the bodies and eating habits of those around them.

There are also certain physical signs of an eating disorder. One of the most important of these is significant weight loss. Doctors may weigh patients as a way of monitoring health. If a person has lost a lot of weight in a short period of time, a doctor is obligated to ask why. It could be a sign of serious disease, but it could also result from a change in eating habits.

Eating disorders can also make it difficult for a person to regulate body temperature. The human body runs on food as fuel. When a person eats a meal or a snack, that food is broken down by the digestive system and absorbed. Carbohydrates in the foods a person consumes are broken down into glucose. This glucose is released into the bloodstream and travels around the body, fueling the brain, the heart, the muscles, and all of the other organs. An eating disorder takes away that fuel, forcing the body to instead break down existing muscles and fat in order to keep itself running. As the body loses fat, it's losing part of what protects it from the cold. This means people with eating disorders are often cold, even when it's warm outside.

Eating disorders can also disrupt basic digestive functions and the well-being of the digestive system. The human body is hardwired to vomit in order to get rid of a contaminant. That's why people might feel unwell for several days while experiencing food poisoning. The body is fighting to get itself well again by purging what's bothering it. But people aren't meant to vomit in nonemergency situations. Many who struggle with bulimia might have acid reflux caused by long-term damage to the esophagus. This damage can eventually become so significant that the esophagus tears or even ruptures. Many who suffer from an eating disorder have frequent stomach cramps or nausea. Using laxatives to stimulate a bowel movement can also cause long-term damage to the body. Many abuse laxatives as a way to rush food out of the body before it can be absorbed and turned into fat. Others feel the urge to eliminate waste as quickly as possible because food, and the resulting waste, are heavy. Writer Courtney Enlow said in a 2017 article, "I wasn't just drawn to bulimia and laxatives because I wanted to be thinner; I felt a compulsive need to completely remove from my body anything but the parts it needed to run."[20]

> "I wasn't just drawn to bulimia and laxatives because I wanted to be thinner; I felt a compulsive need to completely remove from my body anything but the parts it needed to run."[20]
>
> – Writer Courtney Enlow

Many laxatives work by pulling moisture into the colon. That means when the waste is eliminated, so is that moisture. Excessive use of laxatives can lead to severe dehydration, which can damage the kidneys or cause the bowels to stop functioning normally altogether. In the long term, laxative abuse can lead to chronic constipation. The muscles in the lower intestine weaken and don't contract the way they should to move waste through the bowel.

Without enough food to fuel the brain, it often becomes difficult to concentrate at school or work. A person can become dizzy or even faint at times. Malnutrition can slow the heart rate, lower potassium levels, lead to anemia (a reduction of healthy red blood cells), or cause changes to hormone levels or thyroid activity. These symptoms can affect a person's ability to heal from a wound or fight illness. The menstrual cycle might become irregular or stop altogether.

A person's appearance can also be affected. Excessive vomiting can cause damage to the teeth, often resulting in cavities or tooth loss.

**Eating disorders have physical effects on the body. The damage is sometimes permanent.**

Hair and nails can become dry and brittle. A person's skin can also dry out or appear discolored.

A doctor seeing any number of these characteristics or changes in behavior might become concerned and decide to take action. A family member might notice significant changes to a loved one. Friends might become concerned as a person withdraws and starts to isolate himself. Or a person may realize herself that she is in danger. The first step toward diagnosis in many cases is a visit to a doctor or mental health professional.

## SEEING A DOCTOR

Being diagnosed with an eating disorder is multilayered and requires many steps. The first step is often being examined by a physician. For this visit, it might help to bring along a friend or family member to help listen and communicate a patient's needs more effectively. It can also help to write down specific questions beforehand and take notes during the visit. Dr. Leslie Sanders of the Eating Disorders Program of Goryeb Children's Center says, "We know that the sooner someone seeks help (for an eating disorder) the more likely they are to recover."[21]

> "We know that the sooner someone seeks help (for an eating disorder) the more likely they are to recover."[21]
>
> – Dr. Leslie Sanders, doctor at the Eating Disorders Program of Goryeb Children's Center

A doctor who listens and understands a patient's concerns will want to first assess the patient's physical well-being. If she suspects that an eating disorder might be present, she'll ask some questions relating to behavior. Some of these questions will feel very personal and invasive. A doctor might ask a patient if she is dissatisfied with her body size, if she ever makes herself vomit, if her weight affects how she thinks about herself, or whether she feels food dominates her life. These are just a few of the standard questions in assessing whether or not a person has an eating disorder. Doctors will also run blood tests to determine what parts of the body are being affected. An eating disorder can take a serious toll on some of the body's basic functions, and a doctor needs to make sure a patient is not in immediate danger. If a patient is severely dehydrated or otherwise extremely ill, he might need to spend a night or two in the hospital receiving intravenous fluids. While in the hospital, he will likely get a visit from a psychiatrist to determine his mental and emotional well-being

**Talking with a doctor or mental health professional is an important step in recovering from an eating disorder. A professional can help develop a treatment plan based on the patient's needs.**

and begin to talk through some treatment options. This is all determined by the severity of a person's condition. In certain extremely severe cases, a patient may be referred to an inpatient treatment program in order to receive immediate, sometimes lifesaving care. This means a long-term stay in a hospital or mental health facility specializing in the treatment of eating disorders. There, a person will receive a diagnosis and long-term treatment plan.

Some eating disorders, like binge-eating disorder, are not often characterized by significant weight loss. A person can have an eating disorder and not be in immediate danger but still need help. A doctor might run some tests and determine that the patient is physically healthy but struggling emotionally and mentally. The patient might have some habits that could evolve into a physically debilitating issue. The next step in this case is a visit with a mental health professional to provide a diagnosis. Even if a doctor is able to make an official diagnosis, he will very often refer patients to a mental health professional for counseling and additional support.

## VISITING A MENTAL HEALTH PROFESSIONAL

There are many types of mental health professionals. Psychiatrists are medical doctors who specialize in mental disorders and can provide a diagnosis. They will often order blood tests if another doctor hasn't already. They might also prescribe some medications, such as an antidepressant or anti-anxiety medication, since these conditions are often linked to eating disorders. Psychologists are high-level experts in mental health, but not medical doctors. A psychologist works one-on-one with patients. Psychologists can make an official diagnosis as well. Some types of therapists, counselors, social workers, and nurses with advanced training can also make an official diagnosis with a patient. Others might offer counseling but need to work in coordination with a psychiatrist or psychologist to make an official diagnosis. Mental health care options are often determined by a person's health insurance coverage, treatment available in the area, and personal preference toward one type of treatment or another.

All mental health professionals start out with a patient by doing a psychological evaluation. This might include a basic questionnaire, a one-on-one informal chat with a patient, a more in-depth psychological test, or a period of observation. For younger patients or someone who requires additional support, a professional might talk to parents or teachers to better understand the patient's common behaviors or habits. Professionals look for signs of an eating disorder. According to clinical psychologist Rachel Goldman, "If someone is trying to lose weight, has body image issues, or [has] any kind of disordered thoughts around eating and weight, they may be more hesitant to eat in front of other people."[22] This is just one of the signs that a mental health professional might look for.

Mental health professionals use the collected information to develop a diagnosis. They will then sit down with the patient—and sometimes the patient's family—to work out a treatment plan.

> "If someone is trying to lose weight, has body image issues, or [has] any kind of disordered thoughts around eating and weight, they may be more hesitant to eat in front of other people."[22]
>
> – Clinical psychologist Rachel Goldman on some of the signs of an eating disorder

If a person is diagnosed with an eating disorder, she may be looking at a few additional diagnoses. Eating disorders are often tied to anxiety disorders, depression, PTSD, substance abuse, or a type of personality disorder, like borderline personality disorder. If a mental health professional determines that a patient is struggling with an additional condition, he will factor that into the treatment plan as well. The existence of more than one serious condition in a single patient is known as comorbidity.

## HANDLING A DIAGNOSIS

Many people feel relieved after receiving a diagnosis for a serious mental health condition. It can be comforting to know the underlying cause of certain behaviors and emotions. Others might feel afraid or resentful, because it can be difficult to feel that there's something wrong with them. Some feel ashamed and are afraid of being judged or ostracized. Everyone's experience is different, and that's why it's important to establish a good, honest relationship with the mental health professional in charge of one's care. No matter what kind of emotion a person is feeling, it can be helpful to talk about it.

Eating disorders often result in a person feeling alone and isolated. After a diagnosis, it can be helpful to reestablish relationships with friends and family who care about one's well-being as treatment preparations are made. "When you're sick," says Kimberly Neil, who has struggled with an eating disorder since the age of eleven, "people expect you to get better. This is why compassion is essential."[23]

## BODY-FOCUSED REPETITIVE BEHAVIORS

Eating disorders are tied to a lack of impulse control, and because of this, there are certain behaviors that those with eating disorders often experience. A few of these behaviors are trichotillomania, dermatillomania, and onychophagia. Trichotillomania is the compulsion to pull out one's own hair. Dermatillomania is picking at the skin. Onychophagia is a compulsion to bite one's nails down into the nail bed. Plucking a hair, picking at a pimple, or nibbling at a fingernail on occasion is totally normal. But when the activity becomes uncontrollable, that's when it becomes what's known as a body-focused repetitive behavior.

Body-focused repetitive behaviors can affect people at any age and affect about 3 percent of the population. They are often treated as part of therapy that addresses a larger issue, such as anxiety or an obsessive-compulsive disorder. It is possible to have a body-focused repetitive behavior without having an eating disorder. But they are often related.

# CHAPTER **THREE**

# WHAT IS LIFE LIKE WITH AN EATING DISORDER?

Everyone has a unique eating style. Some people eat because it's time and they're hungry. They aren't afraid to grab a slice of pizza or a food truck burrito on the run. Others cherish mealtimes as a way of honoring their heritage or celebrating time with family. There are people who love food and the preparation of it. They enjoy the smell and feel of a freshly picked tomato and making that tomato into a tangy sauce, carefully adding just the right amount of salt and cream. But the relationship with food and eating is different for people with eating disorders. In some ways, it's all-encompassing. They think about it all the time. In other ways, they resent it. Maura Preszler developed an eating disorder in eighth grade. Food dominated her life during her early struggles with anorexia: "I allowed myself 100 or 200 calories a day. If I survived the day on 100 calories, I considered it to be a good day."[24]

Food isn't a celebration to someone with an eating disorder. It is not fuel to get through the day. Food is a curse, weakness, or burden.

**Many people enjoy food. But struggling with an eating disorder can make this joy seem impossible.**

Having an eating disorder means not having a normal, enjoyable relationship with food. It can mean being angry and resentful toward one's own body when it doesn't meet a specific standard. This can affect how some people live their lives every day. Living with an eating disorder can be extremely challenging, affecting school, work, and relationships with others.

## DAILY LIFE AROUND FOOD

Across the broad spectrum of eating disorders, there are a lot of different attitudes toward food. Anorexia is an avoidance of food due to fear of gaining weight. Bulimia and binge-eating disorder both include an overconsumption of food. Both also often result in feelings of guilt when sufferers do eat. In any eating disorder, sufferers become so focused on food that other things in life don't matter as much in comparison.

"Living with eating disorder thinking means actively ignoring a voice in my head that tells me it's dangerous to have a favorite restaurant (Tanoreen in Brooklyn) or to lick my lips while savoring sumac shredded chicken. . . . It's never being able to engage in conversations with other women—and, boy are there many—about losing weight or trying out a fad diet," says Lisa Fogarty, whose struggles with anorexia have continued into adulthood.[25]

Much of American culture is centered around food. Holidays like Thanksgiving and Christmas provide an overabundance of food in many households. People try to outdo each other's Super Bowl parties year after year, providing a bigger and bigger spread. There are lively summer barbecues, buffets, and banquets tied to weddings, funerals, christenings, birthdays, and other common events. Americans love to eat. They love a celebration of abundance. They love providing for their families and showing their fondness through food. When food is so central to everything, people who suffer from eating disorders can feel alienated.

Americans also embrace fitness and the diet industry. They enjoy TV shows like *The Biggest Loser*, where contestants compete to lose the most weight for a cash prize. After its debut in 2004, the show garnered high ratings and a large viewership, lasting seventeen seasons. Seeing the before-and-after effects of weight loss make many people feel hopeful that they can one day achieve similar results. They might get frustrated when those results don't come as easily as they do on TV.

Because of American food culture and an ongoing obsession with dieting, fitness, and attaining an "ideal" body, everyday life around food can be tough to navigate for someone with an eating disorder. A person might feel like all of his food decisions are under scrutiny by others. Just sitting down to lunch in a school cafeteria can be difficult, even if someone is actively experiencing feelings of hunger. A student might feel insecure about the amount of food on her plate, or her food

> "[People with eating disorders] get anxious about how that slice of pizza will damage our body and we worry we look disgusting as we take a bite of it. We become nervous about letting people see us eat."[26]
>
> – Gina M. Florio, on living with binge-eating disorder

choices, or how she'll look eating. This may evolve into avoiding eating altogether. A person may start to feel isolated from friends and family as he works to avoid eating. According to Gina Florio, who has battled binge-eating disorder since high school, "[People with eating disorders] get anxious about how that slice of pizza will damage our body and we worry we look disgusting as we take a bite of it. We become nervous about letting people see us eat."[26]

Many with eating disorders isolate themselves even more when someone asks them why they don't seem hungry or tries to force them to eat. This can make the situation worse. "In college, I used to expect this inquiry any time I ate dinner with someone outside my circle of friends. In fact, I didn't just hear it from my classmates, but also from dining hall employees—they'd raise their eyebrows at my plate of carrot sticks and scoop of hummus and ask, 'That's all you're getting?'" said De Elizabeth, writing on her experiences with anorexia.[27]

Eventually, as the disorder takes hold, people may lose touch with some of the everyday instincts of eating. They might not notice hunger pangs, ignore them, or even revel in them because it feels like they're in control. Many develop a deep-seated fear of food that can last for years. Some people are never able to let go of that fear, and it lasts the rest of their lives.

## THE STRUGGLE FOR "HEALTHY"

*Healthy* has become a complicated term. Food manufacturers label certain products as healthy or healthier than some alternatives. This term appears in headlines and dieting books, on posters in doctors' waiting rooms, and in gym membership pamphlets. *Healthy* is everywhere and often misused. In a 2016 article for the *Washington Post*, writer Michael Ruhlman wrote about the habit of kale salads and similar trendy foods being called healthy. He wrote that kale salads are nutritious, but if all a person ate was kale salads, she would eventually become sick. This is often where someone with an eating disorder will struggle. If eating certain foods or eating excessively is seen as unhealthy, as is often popularized by diet culture, then not eating enough or at all is sometimes understood to be healthy. Eating disorders blur the line between healthy and unhealthy. This makes it difficult for someone who is struggling with an eating disorder to recognize his behavior as abnormal. Unhealthy eating behaviors and excessive physical activity can seem normal. This can make going to the doctor feel unnecessary, as well.

Doctors have the responsibility to care for those who are sick, but many medical professionals still struggle to fully understand and care

**Americans' obsession with dieting and healthy foods makes it hard to make balanced food choices. An eating disorder can make this balance even harder.**

for someone with an eating disorder. Many doctors have preconceived notions of what healthy looks like. They still use the body mass index (BMI) scale, which catalogs patients as underweight, normal weight, overweight, and obese based on height and weight statistics. However, this practice is considered outdated by some medical experts. Cardiovascular researcher for the Mayo Clinic Jose Medina-Inojosa believes that several more factors should be considered, like how fat is distributed in the body and what that means to future health concerns. Furthermore, many doctors are not well trained to recognize, diagnose, and provide adequate support for someone with an eating disorder. A doctor might see a patient whose weight and height categorizes her as obese and recommend "diet and exercise" as a solution. However, the doctor might not think to ask a few questions about the patient's eating habits. These questions might reveal that she struggles with binge-eating disorder. Now this patient might relapse into past disordered habits or adopt new ones to achieve doctor-recommended weight loss. "In an office that may be seeing far more issues with obesity than other more identifiable eating disorders, clinicians may forget to ask about eating habits, and they may not have had the opportunity to develop sensitivity and awareness regarding neutral language around healthy eating and weight," said psychiatrist Evelyn Attia. "These things are extremely important to an individual who is seeking help for eating problems."[28]

"Clinicians may forget to ask about eating habits, and they may not have had the opportunity to develop sensitivity and awareness regarding neutral language around healthy eating and weight."[28]

– Evelyn Attia, psychiatrist

This is why it is often so complicated and difficult to get help for an eating disorder. Many people live with these conditions for years without seeking help. They might not understand that there's anything wrong with their eating or exercise habits. They might avoid going to see a doctor altogether. Someone who is aware that some of his behaviors are indicative of a problem still has to face the risk of a medical professional making damaging remarks. Rosemary Donahue, who has struggled with bulimia since her teens, was once weighed by a nurse who commented, "You're lucky. I wish I weighed the same."[29] Someone not struggling with an eating disorder might appreciate this as a compliment. For others, it's a careless remark that could undo years of recovery. Situations like this are a daily struggle for many with eating disorders.

Fitness and its connection to health also takes on a different context. The weight loss philosophy of input/output, where a person must work

**Misunderstandings about the connection between fitness and weight loss can lead to dangerous behaviors. Setting goals other than weight loss, such as learning a new activity or running a certain distance, can be more beneficial.**

off the calories in anything she consumes in order to maintain her weight, is popular with many personal trainers and other fitness professionals. It assumes that weight gain is the result of consuming more calories than are being burned through exercise or everyday activities, but weight loss is more complicated than that. Age, disease, metabolism, medications, genetics, and other factors play into how quickly and effectively someone gains or loses fat cells. Assuming that this one method is universally effective pushes a lot of people to work harder to lose weight, and sometimes that hard work slips into eating disorder territory. Many people assume that any weight loss is good weight loss, and this idea is helped along by the diet industry and popular media. If cutting back to a 1,200-calories-a-day routine and running several miles each morning helps a person lose 4 pounds (1.8 kg) in a month, how many pounds could he lose if he cut back to only 600 calories daily? Weight loss is often portrayed as an ultimate good no matter how it's achieved. Living every day in a world where experts promote weight loss at any cost is detrimental to someone with an eating disorder.

Social media has helped to usher in a new era of dieting in which anyone on Instagram can share and promote their own weight loss strategies. Frequent celebrity spokeswoman Kim Kardashian was criticized in 2018 for posting an ad on her Instagram for appetite suppressant lollipops meant to aid in weight loss. "This promotes an unhealthy and damaging relationship with food and we absolutely must take a stand against anything that could be damaging to people online,"

## ALL MUSCLE, NO FAT

Hockey player Logan Davis was a starter goalie for the Ohio State Buckeyes when he first decided to get himself into peak physical condition to impress his coaches. To Davis, this meant all muscle and no fat. He started to work out and watch what he was eating. When he started to see results, he worked harder. Soon, he was eating only about 500 calories a day. This was only about 17 percent of the recommended calorie intake (3,000 calories) for someone his age who is active in sports. He dropped 30 pounds (14 kg).

Anorexia and other disorders among male athletes have become more common. According to NEDA, around 33 percent of male athletes involved in sports such as bodybuilding, gymnastics, and swimming will struggle with an eating disorder. Weight-class sports like wrestling and rowing often push athletes to fit into specific weight guidelines. These athletes will resort to using laxatives and diuretics, or they may try to lose water weight quickly by using saunas. Because eating disorders are often overlooked in men's sports, coaches aren't trained in recognizing disordered behavior in athletes. They might not notice certain behaviors until an athlete is in serious danger.

said activist Liam Hackett.[30] Actress Jameela Jamil, an outspoken advocate of body positivity and acceptance, also spoke out in frustration. Many were afraid that young people would be encouraged to participate in disordered behaviors.

## NAVIGATING LIFE AROUND A DISORDER

One of the biggest challenges that someone with an eating disorder must face is keeping up with all of the other things that life requires: having a job, maintaining friendships and family relationships, getting to class, and more. As with any mental health condition, an eating disorder can present everyday challenges. Some jobs require lunch meetings or other commitments where food is a factor. This can be difficult for someone who struggles to eat normally around others. An eating disorder can also be a distraction, putting people in a situation where all they can concentrate on is eating or not eating. James, a contributor on the Beat Eating Disorders website, said, "Over the years when I suffered with anorexia, I was so preoccupied with avoiding food, compulsively exercising and abusing laxatives in order to lose weight that my eating disorder eventually became much more important and time-consuming than work."[31]

Some people may eventually need to take a leave of absence from work to take time for recovery, which can delay career aspirations or affect a raise or a promotion. They may feel as if their personal lives are on display for others at work when they have to talk to a boss or HR manager about managing their eating disorder in the workplace. Someone who works for an hourly wage and doesn't have paid time off may find herself unable to pay her bills during the recovery time. She may struggle to pay for treatment or regular visits with her care team. This could lead to a relapse for someone who is actively seeking treatment.

Students face similar consequences at school. According to the Eating Disorder Hope website, 2.7 percent of teens aged thirteen through eighteen struggle with eating disorders. An eating disorder can affect a student's school schedule, social activities, and jobs, making many teens reluctant to seek help. They may fear judgment if word of their disorder gets out. They might find themselves struggling to maintain their grades, even losing scholarships or a job they require to cover tuition. Many students are reluctant to walk away from school and scholarships because they may never have that kind of opportunity again. Hannah Durbin was waiting for the "perfect" time to seek treatment for her eating disorder. Ultimately, she realized the perfect time would never come. She was not fully experiencing life in college, so she decided to take some time off and seek treatment. "A college education is incredibly valuable, but your life is priceless. . . . If a few months of treatment could give me an eternity of freedom, then I needed to do it. I am so grateful I chose treatment. It was hard, but missing out on life would have been harder."[32]

Certain cases will allow for a student to take a leave of absence to deal with illness and focus on recovery. Since eating disorders are linked to perfectionism and high achievement in students, taking time away may add to a student's stress. But for many, it's the right choice. "During my junior year, I had an assessment at a treatment center near my school," said Dena Angela, who struggled with anorexia nervosa and orthorexia. "Seven months of intensive treatment later, I moved home for a semester. What I learned from my experience is that taking a break from school is heartbreaking at the moment that it's happening, but it is the best thing you will ever do for yourself. . . . I will always feel sad that I lost three years of my college experience to my eating disorder. I will never regret sacrificing one year of my college experience for recovery."[33]

Eating disorders are often described as lonely. Many sufferers find themselves withdrawing socially from friends and family because food-related social events make them feel anxious. They might find that it's easier to avoid an outing altogether than to face questions about why they aren't hungry.

> "I will always feel sad that I lost three years of my college experience to my eating disorder. I will never regret sacrificing one year of my college experience for recovery."[33]
>
> *– Dena Angela, on taking a break from school to battle anorexia*

Some encounter issues with dating and intimate relationships. Sharing information about an eating disorder is very personal, and some people aren't comfortable being upfront about mental health issues with someone new. Many potential partners might not understand or might be critical and judgmental. Relationships can lead to heightened awareness of another person's body or personal habits. Many who suffer from eating disorders work to avoid situations like these. Not dating at all might seem easier in the end. Unfortunately, this will only increase the feelings of isolation that can come with an eating disorder.

Many who struggle with an eating disorder have trouble looking at other people's bodies without judgment. They might keep a close watch on what others are eating and wearing. This can trickle down to children and other younger family members, triggering similar behavior in them. "Over time, my parents taught me that I should decide what to eat with my brain, not my stomach," said Suzannah Weiss. "So eventually, my

**Relatives can teach about healthy eating, but they also can pass on negative feelings toward food. Even comments about wanting to lose weight can establish negative thoughts in children.**

stomach just gave up."[34] Weiss's parents controlled her eating as a child, putting her on her first diet when she was thirteen years old. She feels that their influence led to her struggle with anorexia.

An older family member with an eating disorder may believe he's helping a young person to live a healthier life and not realize it's causing harm. Preoccupation with diet and exercise might make it difficult for a parent to do something as simple as share an ice cream cone with a child. The parent might feel uncomfortable celebrating a birthday party or other special occasion due to concerns about food. Having a normal life around others feels like a challenge and a daily struggle for people with eating disorders.

A food-focused society in which dieting is the norm can feel like a minefield for people with eating disorders. Seeking out and succeeding at treatment might feel like just another obstacle, rather than a relief. But if someone is willing to take the first step to get help, treatment is possible.

## WOMEN'S GYMNASTICS AND THE DRIVE FOR PERFECTION

In 2013, a few years before she would break records and win gold at the 2016 Olympics, Simone Biles was struggling. After a fall on the uneven bars and a stumble in her floor routine, she overheard an opposing team's coach say, "You know why [she] crashed? Because she's too fat, that's why." In her 2016 memoir, Biles recounted that she felt humiliated by the comment. There is a drive among female gymnasts to win at any cost, and sometimes this can result in an eating disorder.

At the peak of their careers, female gymnasts are usually in their teens or early twenties, and the pressure for them to lose weight to stay competitive is constant. In her own memoir, gymnast Jennifer Sey recalls being addicted to laxatives and engaging in bingeing and purging behaviors. She endured humiliating comments from coaches about being too fat. Gymnast Christy Henrich passed away at the age of twenty-two from multiple organ failure due to her eating disorder struggle in 1994. She had dropped to less than 60 pounds (27 kg). As sexual abuse allegations in US women's gymnastics came to light in 2018, so did accusations against former US women's team coaches Bela and Marta Karolyi. They were accused of habitually starving the athletes in their care and body shaming them. The pair have since retired, and many feel hopeful that the future will bring about a healthier standard for women's gymnastics.

Quoted in Simone Biles, Courage to Soar: A Body in Motion, A Life in Balance. New York: HarperCollins, 2016.

CHAPTER
**FOUR**

# HOW ARE EATING DISORDERS TREATED?

One popular myth about eating disorders is that a person can just realize they're in danger, cut out bad habits, and eat normally again. Some people think that it's just a type of extreme diet. And it's true that many people can decide one day to go on a diet, reach their goals, and live a healthy life on their terms. For people with eating disorders, however, chronic dieting can become a way of life. Food becomes an all-encompassing obsession that takes over their life, makes them sick, and fills every moment with thoughts of controlling their food intake. In the same way that no one can tell a depressed person to just "cheer up" or an anxious person to "relax," no one can tell a person with an eating disorder to simply eat or not eat. According to an article on eating disorder treatment website Mirror Mirror, "Eating disorders are not simply about choice, there is a significant mental component and biological basis to the disorder which is preventing the sufferer from eating normally."[35]

**People often relapse while seeking treatment. Many treatment plans discuss how to prevent and recover from relapses.**

Treating an eating disorder is a complicated, long-term process, even when treatment is successful. Some people are never truly cured. An eating disorder can affect a person for the rest of her life. This is why finding the most comprehensive treatment is important.

## THE FIRST STEPS TOWARD GETTING BETTER

Once an eating disorder is diagnosed, the next step is finding the right treatment plan. Treatment depends on individual needs and severity of a person's condition. Usually, the best course of treatment will be determined by a doctor or mental health professional. "Even if you technically know what eating disorders are, it can be difficult to tell if you actually have one," says Ashley Benoit of *Teen Vogue*.[36]

Severe eating disorder cases often leave patients in weak physical condition, and a doctor's first goal is to treat any physical complications. This often means spending some time in the hospital while exploring inpatient care options. Inpatient clinics that specialize in eating disorders provide basic medical care while working with patients to help them achieve and maintain a healthier weight. The most severe cases are usually patients with anorexia or bulimia, but other types of eating disorders can also have dangerous consequences and require inpatient treatment. Inpatient care will normally be recommended for any individual who is in immediate need of medical intervention, has a complication with another serious medical condition like diabetes, or is struggling with mental stability. Patients with mental instability show signs that they might be at risk of harming themselves and might struggle to make sound decisions for care on their own behalf. "Those living with an eating disorder and a second comorbid condition like depression, may find that their depressive symptoms make them unable to effectively engage in lower levels of eating disorder care," according to the Walden Behavioral Care program, which offers inpatient treatment for eating disorders. This means that these individuals might struggle with treatment that they are responsible for managing on their own, as with an outpatient program. "These individuals may need to be hospitalized in order to stabilize depression symptoms before they can return to a lower level of care."[37]

While in a hospital or inpatient facility, patients will also spend time with one or more mental health professionals who are responsible for their treatment. One-on-one therapy sessions take place as frequently as caregivers feel is necessary. Programs will often offer group therapy overseen by a professional, in which groups of patients can spend time together, talking through some of the issues they're facing. "One of the most empowering aspects of group therapy is that it brings to light the fact that you are not alone in your struggle," says therapist Margot Rittenhouse.[38]

> "One of the most empowering aspects of group therapy is that it brings to light the fact that you are not alone in your struggle.[38]
>
> – *Margot Rittenhouse, therapist*

Inpatient care also involves relearning eating habits with the help of a nutritionist or dietician. The goal of this is working toward a healthy weight while learning how to manage food again. Many people who struggle with eating disorders have simply lost touch with the basics of healthy eating, shopping for food, and meal preparation. Feeding themselves well doesn't feel normal anymore. Sessions with a dietician might include some training in food preparation, meal planning, and establishing some healthier eating patterns. This prepares patients to manage their care outside of inpatient treatment. "For both adults and adolescents with eating disorders, those families who prioritize and make the time for regular meal planning and shopping make better progress in treatment," says psychotherapist Lauren Muhlheim.[39]

Patients often have to learn how to eat three meals a day in addition to snacks. They'll learn how to respond to their feelings of hunger in a positive way again. Patients will learn about some of the physical effects that different eating habits are having on their bodies. They'll learn some strategies for avoiding bingeing or purging behaviors.

How long a patient stays in an inpatient treatment center is determined by need. In general, each individual requires different levels and types of support. Unique needs may extend a person's stay. Once people leave an inpatient program, their work needs to be continued with patience, perseverance, and support. They must continue to see a doctor regularly so that their health can be monitored. They'll continue mental health treatment, whether they spend time with a psychotherapist in one-on-one sessions, go to group therapy, or do a combination of these things.

Inpatient care isn't the only option. In some cases, the cost of inpatient treatment is high. Even just a short hospital stay can be very expensive. When inpatient care is not necessary or possible, outpatient

## STRATEGIES FOR AFFORDING TREATMENT

The cost of treatment can be a huge roadblock for many suffering from an eating disorder. Inpatient treatment programs can cost an average of $30,000 a month, but long-term treatment is often not covered by health insurance benefits. While many factors might affect a person's choice not to seek professional help, cost is high on the list. Some people might need to explore a few different options before finding the right financial strategy.

The Eating Disorder Hope site recommends several ways to find help, like finding a research program run by a university or hospital. The University of California, San Diego, has one such program. It offers care, treatment, and low-cost housing for participants. They also suggest looking for nonprofit organizations that provide treatment scholarships or sliding scale pay options. Some, like NEDA, have toll-free helplines for immediate support. University counseling programs might also be an option for students. Most colleges offer counseling services and may offer group counseling for eating disorders. There are also community mental health facilities that offer both inpatient and outpatient care programs at a lower cost than a private facility.

care is often an effective option. Outpatient treatment programs offer counseling and support. These might be a better fit for those who have financial concerns, who cannot miss work or school, or who have family obligations. Rather than living in a facility during treatment, patients in an outpatient program can live at home but attend as many counseling sessions a week as necessary to manage their care. Outpatient centers often provide group therapy, as well. This treatment is often combined with frequent visits to the doctor so that a patient's health can be closely monitored. Outpatient treatment can also include specific meal planning considerations. This treatment often requires the highest levels of support from family members and friends. This ensures that an individual is able to follow the plan and not fall back into old habits. Unhealthy family dynamics can contribute to eating disorders. In these cases, family therapy is often recommended. The goal of family therapy is improving relationships within the family to support the person with an eating disorder. "Without the support of loved ones in your life," says the Eating Disorder Hope website, "you are risking the possibility of being destroyed by your eating disorder."[40]

> "Without the support of loved ones in your life, you are risking the possibility of being destroyed by your eating disorder."[40]
>
> – EatingDisorderHope.com

Less severe, non-life-threatening eating disorder cases will often not require a specific inpatient or outpatient care plan or any time in a hospital. But these individuals will still need a comprehensive treatment plan. This can include visits with a dietitian and mental health professional to address the eating disorder issues and improve mental and physical health. These cases require self-management on the part of patients.

**There are many types of therapy. People's doctors or mental health professionals can help find the best type for them.**

Patients must be sure to attend therapy sessions and ask for help when they feel their behaviors are slipping back into an unhealthy place.

## DIFFERENT TYPES OF THERAPY

Therapy is a different experience for everyone. This is partially because there are a lot of different types of therapy that have been used in the treatment of eating disorders. Sometimes a combination of these types of therapy comes into play.

One of the most common types of therapy is cognitive behavioral therapy (CBT). CBT helps a patient to identify and understand some of her negative thought patterns and learn ways to navigate them in a less destructive manner. This is achieved by talking through feelings with a therapist. The therapist might ask about certain memories or experiences. This type of therapy can be emotionally draining and difficult, as it can bring a lot of pain to the surface. A patient may even cry or get angry. Ultimately, however, experiencing and exploring these emotions will give the patient the awareness to recognize a certain feeling and manage how she responds to it in the future.

Medical nutrition therapy is a type of holistic therapy specific to eating disorders. In this kind of plan, a registered dietician works with a patient to help stabilize his condition, teach and normalize some new habits around food, and rework how he is nourished. It can be used in both inpatient and outpatient care.

Dialectical behavioral therapy (DBT) is a type of CBT psychotherapy that is often used on patients who have extreme emotional reactions to certain circumstances. DBT is used to help patients regulate their emotions in times of extreme stress. Patients learn how to enter into stressful situations more mindfully so that they can handle stressors in a healthier manner. Emotional highs and lows are a big factor in triggering disordered behaviors. DBT was originally developed for people who have borderline personality disorder. Due to its focus on regulating emotions and developing healthy coping mechanisms, professionals have begun using it to treat eating disorders.

There are many other therapy options, as well. Some have mixed degrees of effectiveness, but they can be used to treat eating disorders. Art therapy allows patients to express their feelings through painting or sculpting. Dance movement therapy connects feelings to movement. Equine therapy allows a patient to build an emotional connection with a specially trained horse. Building a bond with an animal can help a patient develop confidence, courage, self-control, and responsibility. Exposure therapy asks patients to face and spend time with the thing they fear. It is most commonly used to treat anxiety but can be used to treat eating disorders.

These and other types of therapy have been used in the treatment of eating disorders in the past. Finding the right type of therapy or combination of therapies is important. "The field of psychotherapy has evolved a lot over the last few decades," says Jennice Vilhauer, a professor at Emory University School of Medicine. "It's no longer what we'd call a one-size-fits-all model."[41]

## THE ROLE OF MEDICATION

In addition to therapy, many who struggle with eating disorders might consider medication as an option. This can be a big decision, as medications often come with side effects. But some side effects can be tolerable if the benefits outweigh them. A licensed medical provider can prescribe medication, and it should only be taken as prescribed. Physicians carefully evaluate a patient's condition before prescribing medications for any mental health issue. Medication is not a cure, but it can help with some of the difficult symptoms of eating disorders. While there is no medication to treat eating disorders specifically, medications can help treat co-occurring mental issues and make it easier to manage an eating disorder. Some common medications typically prescribed to someone with a mental disorder are antidepressants, anti-anxiety medications, mood stabilizers, antipsychotics, and stimulants.

Depression can often co-occur with eating disorders. Depression is typically portrayed as profound sadness, but it can also include a lack of energy, hopeless feelings, inability to concentrate, or a lack of interest in things. Antidepressants generally balance levels of certain neurotransmitters in the brain. Neurotransmitters are chemicals responsible for emotions. This often results in an improved mood, lessening of disturbing feelings, and mental clarity. "Antidepressants aren't a happy pill; they just clear the fog for me," says Lynn Stattuck. "They help clear my vision and enable me to be able to see a little more."[42] Treating underlying depression can help people with an eating disorder to better manage their care.

> "Antidepressants aren't a happy pill; they just clear the fog for me. . . . They help clear my vision and enable me to be able to see a little more."[42]
>
> – Lynn Stattuck

A doctor or mental health professional might also prescribe an anti-anxiety medication. Long-term anti-anxiety medications can help people with chronic conditions. Fast-acting medications are used in case of an anxiety or panic attack. Some anti-anxiety medications work by increasing serotonin levels in the brain. Serotonin is the neurotransmitter that makes people feel happy. Other anti-anxiety medications relieve the symptoms of anxiety, such as muscle stiffness or a feeling of panic. Additionally, some double as antidepressants and help to manage both.

Mood stabilizers are also sometimes prescribed in certain eating disorder cases. These are frequently prescribed for disorders characterized by mood swings. One of these is bipolar disorder, in which a person experiences periods of high-energy elation (mania) followed by severe depression. Bipolar disorder is often linked to novelty-seeking behaviors and struggles with self-control. These can often affect eating behaviors. Mood stabilizers manage extreme brain activity that leads to manic episodes and depression.

**Many patients find success in taking a medication to manage co-occurring disorders. A doctor or mental health professional will help decide if medication would be a good fit.**

In some cases, a patient might be prescribed an antipsychotic medication, which helps to manage psychosis. Psychosis is a loss of contact with reality. This can include hallucinations or delusions. Psychosis can co-occur with an eating disorder. Some antipsychotic medications have been studied for use with anorexic patients as an aid to gaining weight. However, they weren't determined to be effective on their own.

Long-acting simulant medications can treat attention-deficit hyperactivity disorder (ADHD). Stimulants are habit-forming and can be abused. They are not recommended for patients with anorexia, as they can suppress appetite. However, a stimulant called Vyvanse was the first FDA-approved treatment for binge-eating disorder.

Treating an eating disorder with medications can be complicated. Medications often have side effects, and they affect everyone differently. One person can safely take a certain antidepressant and feel its benefits, while another person taking the same dosage may feel worse, become irritable, experience nausea, or even have suicidal thoughts. This is why patients must only take medications as prescribed and communicate concerns with their doctor and mental health professional. Doctors might recommend switching to a different medication or adjusting dosage. It might take a few trial periods to find the right dosage and medication. Most doctors and mental health professionals will recommend regular psychotherapy in addition to a medication or group of medications in order to monitor how a person is feeling and adjust medications as necessary.

Some people don't like the idea of side effects at all, no matter how minor or inconvenient. They might feel like needing a medication is a weakness. Medications may go against their religious beliefs. Others might struggle to pay for medications and try to cut back to save money. And some people worry that certain drugs will cause them to gain weight, putting them back into a difficult situation with an eating disorder. "Possible weight gain is a big reason why I don't want to take [antidepressants]," says concerned eating disorder patient Meghan on the Finding Balance website, "but so are the other side effects, and the fear that things might be worse if I ever stop the medication. I don't know what to do."[43]

## AVOIDING PRO-ANA CONTENT

One of the most important decisions that anyone with an eating disorder must make is to move away from information or ideas that trigger old behaviors. Pro-ana (pro-anorexia), pro-mia (pro-bulimia), and pro-ED (pro-eating disorder) websites, forums, social media, and group chats have become increasingly popular. Given the unhealthy content of such sites, they can be detrimental to the health and emotional well-being of a person in recovery. These groups support and encourage participants to engage in eating disorder behaviors, post images of "goal" bodies, and even offer tips for weight loss. Many seek out these types of groups because eating disorders can be isolating, and a group can provide support and companionship. However, healthy support is the key for recovery and healing. Support that enables unhealthy behavior will not help a person recover.

Using medication is a personal choice and one that should be discussed with a health care team. Some patients can manage their care without medication at all. Others feel better when using medications. Using medication is not a sign of weakness. For many, medications can amount to lifesaving support.

## OTHER WAYS OF STAYING HEALTHY

Eating disorders and related mental conditions often come with triggers. A trigger is something that causes a person to re-experience something traumatic. This can be a smell, a sound, a sensation, or something else entirely. Triggers can reintroduce old behaviors, so many people in recovery for eating disorders work to avoid these things. Many people with eating disorders avoid talking about diets or remove themselves from a conversation where friends or family members are talking about the parts of their bodies they don't like. Many groups engage in these conversations casually, without understanding the damage it can cause. Learning how to say, "Hey, let's talk about something else," leaving an outing early, or scheduling an emergency therapy session might be an important step for someone with an eating disorder. People might turn backwards on the scale when being weighed at the doctor's office so that they don't see the number and feel shame about their weight. They may avoid a family member who is fast to criticize them. They might give up a gym membership, ask a supportive friend to go clothes shopping with them, or adjust another habit that might seem unrelated to someone who isn't struggling. "I stopped subscribing to and buying popular magazines many years ago," says Nica Stepien, who cites women's magazines with "diet" content prominently displayed on the cover as one of her triggers.[44]

Other eating disorder sufferers work on their self-care, learning how to recognize certain feelings and pausing to assess what they need in that moment to cope. This can mean taking a break, taking a nap, meditating, or just writing in a journal for half an hour. Self-care is different for everyone, and part of recovery is learning what constitutes self-care.

One of the most important things people in recovery can do is to be patient and kind with themselves. It can be easy to blame road bumps and relapses on weakness or laziness. Some might feel guilty over the cost of treatment, for making others worry about them, or for missing school or struggling at work. They might blame themselves for the time-consuming, frustrating nature of recovery. But remembering that an eating disorder is a mental condition and not a chosen set of behaviors can do a lot to foster kindness toward oneself. Recovery isn't quick or easy, but it is possible. Support, perseverance, self-compassion, and ongoing awareness are key to finding a way back from an eating disorder.

# SOURCE NOTES

## INTRODUCTION: HEATHER'S STRUGGLE

1. Jen Gunter, "Food, My Frenemy," *The New York Times on Medium*, November 27, 2018. www.medium.com.

2. Quoted in Caroline Rothstein, "17 Stories of Eating-Disorder Survival," *BuzzFeed News*, February 24, 2015. www.buzzfeednews.com

3. Quoted in Ginny Graves, "How to Know If You're Addicted to Exercise," *Self*, September 15, 2014. www.self.com.

4. Kimberly Neil, "What Recovering from an Eating Disorder Is Really Like," *Teen Vogue*, December 9, 2015. www.teenvogue.com.

## CHAPTER 1: WHAT ARE EATING DISORDERS?

5. Emily T. Troscianko, "Taking, Losing, and Letting Go of Control in Anorexia," *Psychology Today*, August 18, 2015. www.psychologytoday.com.

6. Quoted in William Grimes, "Isabelle Caro, Anorexic Model, Dies at 28," *New York Times*, December 30, 2010. www.nytimes.com.

7. Quoted in Jeff Nelson, "Gabourey Sidibe Reveals Battle with Bulimia and Suicidal Thoughts in New Memoir: Listen to an Excerpt from the Book," *People*, May 2, 2017. www.people.com.

8. Quoted in Michael A. Gonzales, "'I Eat to Fill the Void': Janet Jackson Interview," *The Telegraph*, November 22, 2010. www.telegraph.co.uk.

9. Quoted in Stacy Lipson, "Cravings for Baby Powder, and More Tales of Pica," *NBC News*, March 2, 2011. www.nbcnews.com.

10. Quoted in "Survey Finds Disordered Eating Behaviors Among Three out of Four American Women," *UNC School of Medicine*, April 22, 2008. med.unc.edu.

11. Quoted in Korin Miller, "Demi Lovato Shared Her Family History of Bulimia," *Self*, June 28, 2016. www.self.com.

12. Carolyn Coker Ross, "What You Need to Know to Get Better," *National Eating Disorders Association (NEDA)*, n.d. www.nationaleatingdisorders.org.

13. Sharon K. Farber, "Self-Mutilation, Eating Disorders, and Suicide," *Psychology Today*, November 12, 2014. www.psychologytoday.com.

## CHAPTER 2: HOW ARE EATING DISORDERS DIAGNOSED?

14. Quoted in Mark Tran, "Twiggy, Face of 1966, Reveals She Hated How She Looked," *The Guardian*, February 14, 2016. www.theguardian.com.

15. Gerald Russell, "Bulimia Nervosa: An Ominous Variant of Anorexia Nervosa," *US National Library for Medicine*, August 1979. ncbi.nlm.nih.gov.

16. Quoted in Anthony Rivas, "This Is What It's Like Being a Man with an Eating Disorder," *BuzzFeed*, July 20, 2017. www.buzzfeed.com.

17. Luke Knudsen, "Existing as a Trans Person with an Eating Disorder," *NEDA*, 2018. www.nationaleatingdisorders.org.

18. Quoted in Jeanette Beebe, "Black Women Suffer from Eating Disorders, Too," *The Daily Beast*, August 3, 2018. www.thedailybeast.com.

19. Kevin Watson, "The Painful Exhaustion of 'Hiding' My Eating Disorder," *The Mighty*, February 6, 2017. www.themighty.com.

20. Courtney Enlow, "I Went a Month Without Pooping, and It'll Probably Happen Again," *Bustle*, December 21, 2017. www.bustle.com.

21. Quoted in Ashley Benoit, "This Is the Test Doctors Use to Determine If You Might Have an Eating Disorder," *Teen Vogue*, April 27, 2016. www.teenvogue.com.

22. Quoted in Kimberly Truong, "8 Signs It's Time to See a Therapist About Your Eating Disorder," *Self*, January 29, 2019. www.self.com.

23. Kimberly Neil, "What Recovering from an Eating Disorder Is Really Like."

## CHAPTER 3: WHAT IS LIFE LIKE WITH AN EATING DISORDER?

24. Maura Preszler, "I Hate You, Food: My Struggle with Anorexia," *Life Teen*, July 27, 2019. www.lifeteen.com.

25. Lisa Fogarty, "When Anorexics Grow Up," *The New York Times*, January 11, 2018. www.nytimes.com.

26. Gina M. Florio, "What It's Really Like to Live with an Eating Disorder," *Bustle*, September 14, 2016. www.bustle.com.

27. De Elizabeth, "11 Things You Shouldn't Say to an Anorexia Survivor," *Allure*, July 7, 2017. www.allure.com.

28. Quoted in Rosemary Donahue, "What I Wish My Doctor Understood About My Eating Disorder," *Allure*, July 5, 2017. www.allure.com.

29. Donahue, "What I Wish My Doctor Understood About My Eating Disorder."

30. Quoted in Korin Miller, "Kim Kardashian Is Selling 'Appetite Suppressant' Lollipops," *Women's Health*, May 16, 2018. www.womenshealthmag.com.

31. James, "Managing Work and Managing an Eating Disorder Don't Need to Be in Conflict," *Beat Eating Disorders*, October 10, 2017. www.beateatingdisorders.org.uk.

32. Hannah Durbin, "Why It's More Than OK to Take Time Off from School for Eating Disorder Treatment," *The Mighty*, August 3, 2017. www.themighty.com.

33. Dena Angela, "My Eating Disorder Was Taking Away from My College Experience, So I Chose Recovery," *Her Campus*, November 1, 2017. www.hercampus.com.

34. Suzannah Weiss, "6 Ways My Parents Unintentionally Taught Me Disordered Eating," *Everyday Feminism*, September 16, 2016, www.everydayfeminism.com.

# SOURCE NOTES CONTINUED

## CHAPTER 4: HOW ARE EATING DISORDERS TREATED?

35. Colleen Thompson and Tabitha Farrar, "Approaching Someone with an Eating Disorder," *Mirror Mirror*, 2014. www.mirror-mirror.org.

36. Benoit, "This Is the Test Doctors Use to Determine If You Might Have an Eating Disorder."

37. Pat Jones, "5 Common Signs That Could Indicate the Need for Inpatient Eating Disorder Care," *Walden Behavioral Care*, June 3, 2019. www.waldeneatingdisorders.com.

38. Margot Rittenhouse, "Group Therapy in Eating Disorder Treatment and What to Expect," *Eating Disorder Hope*, September 13, 2017. www.eatingdisorderhope.com.

39. Lauren Muhlheim, "Meal Planning for Eating Disorder Recovery," *verywellmind*, December 25, 2018. www.verywellmind.com.

40. Crystal Karges and Jacquelyn Ekern, "How Do I Tell My Parents That I Have an Eating Disorder?" *Eating Disorder Hope*, March 14, 2013. www.eatingdisorderhope.com.

41. Quoted in Kirstin Fawcett, "What Kind of Therapist—and Which Type of Therapy—Is Right for You?" *US News & World Report*, November 26, 2014. http://health.usnews.com.

42. Quoted in Sarah Klein, "11 Things Only Someone on Antidepressants Understands," *Prevention*, November 30, 2015. www.prevention.com.

43. Quoted in FB Team, "Afraid of Weight Gain from Antidepressants," *Finding Balance*, December 12, 2012. www.findingbalance.com.

44. Nica Stepien, "Coping with Triggers: 'I Didn't Ask to Feel This!'" *Eating Recovery Center*, May 11, 2018. www.eatingrecoverycenter.com.

# FOR FURTHER RESEARCH

## BOOKS

Carrie Arnold, *Decoding Anorexia*. New York: Routledge, 2012.

Racquel Foran, *Living with Eating Disorders*. Minneapolis, MN: Abdo Publishing, 2014.

Katie Green, *Lighter Than My Shadow*. St. Louis, MO: Lion Forge, 2017.

Don Nardo, *Teens and Eating Disorders*. San Diego, CA: ReferencePoint Press, 2017.

Peggy J. Parks, *Bulimia*. San Diego, CA: ReferencePoint Press, 2013.

## INTERNET SOURCES

Emily Deans, "A History of Eating Disorders," *Psychology Today*, December 11, 2011. www.psychologytoday.com.

Jaquelyn Ekern, "Online Eating Disorder Support Groups," *Eating Disorder Hope*, November 2, 2018. www.eatingdisorderhope.com.

"Find a Therapist," *Psychology Today*, n.d. www.psychologytoday.com.

Ed. D'Arcy Lyness, "Eating Disorders," *KidsHealth from Nemours*, January 2019. http://kidshealth.org.

Mayo Clinic Staff, "Eating Disorders," *Mayo Clinic*, February 22, 2018. www.mayoclinic.org.

# WEBSITES

**The Center for Eating Disorders at Sheppard Pratt**
www.eatingdisorder.org

This site includes information about a treatment center, along with resources such as an online self-assessment.

**Eating Disorder Hope**
www.eatingdisorderhope.com

This organization shares information on eating disorders and includes first-person insight through helpful articles.

**National Eating Disorders Association**
www.nationaleatingdisorders.org

This nonprofit organization offers support, guidance, and valuable information to individuals affected by eating disorders and their families.

# INDEX

affording treatment, 60

Alaska Natives, 31

American Psychiatric Association (APA), 16

Angela, Dena, 52–53

anorexia nervosa, 9, 10–14, 16, 19, 21, 26–30, 42–46, 50, 51–54, 58, 67, 68

avoidant/restrictive food intake disorder (ARFID), 18–19

Beat Eating Disorders, 51

Benoit, Ashley, 57–58

Biggest Loser, The, 44–45

Biles, Simone, 55

binge-eating disorder, 4–9, 15–17, 23, 31, 38–39, 43–45, 47–48, 66–67

Binge-Eating Disorder Association, 9

bingeing, 28, 32, 55, 60

body-focused repetitive behaviors
dermatillomania, 41
onychophagia, 41
trichotillomania, 41

body image, 4, 10, 19, 32, 40

body mass index (BMI) scale, 47

body positivity, 19, 51

body shaming, 40–41, 53, 55

body temperature, 9, 12–13, 34

bulimia nervosa, 13–16, 21, 23, 28–29, 30–35, 43–44, 48, 58, 68

BuzzFeed, 6–7, 30

Byron, Lord, 12

cabbage soup diet, 25

carbohydrates, 33, 34

Caro, Isabelle, 13

Carpenter, Karen, 13

causes of eating disorders
genetics, 20–21
trauma, 22–23

clothing, 12, 32

comorbid conditions
anxiety, 8, 11, 14, 18, 21, 33, 39, 40, 41, 56, 64–65
bipolar disorder, 14, 65
borderline personality disorder, 14, 40, 63
depression, 8, 11, 13, 14, 16, 18, 21, 39, 40, 56, 58, 64–65, 67
obsessive-compulsive disorder, 11, 41
post-traumatic stress disorder (PTSD), 23, 40
schizophrenia, 17
substance abuse, 11, 14, 40

control, 6–8, 11–12, 13, 15–16, 22, 23–25, 31, 32, 41, 46, 54, 56, 64–65

Danzinger, Lucy, 19

dating, 53

diabetes, 16, 20, 52, 58

diabulimia, 20

diagnosing eating disorders, 16, 19, 29–31, 32–36, 37–41, 47

Diagnostic and Statistical Manual of Mental Disorders, 5th Edition (DSM-5), 32

diet industry, 23–25, 44, 49

digestive system, 14, 16, 17, 34

disordered eating, 6–7, 19–20, 21, 25, 30

Eating Disorder Hope, 52, 60, 61
Elizabeth, De, 45–46
emotional eating, 22, 32
esophagus, 34
exercise addiction, 7, 8
exercising, 7, 9, 11, 19, 23, 32, 47, 48–49, 54

food in American culture, 44, 45

Goryeb Children's Center, 37
gymnastics, 50, 55

Hackett, Liam, 50–51
hair, 12–13, 17, 28, 36, 41
history of eating disorders, 26, 28–30
hormones, 20, 35
hospitalization, 28, 37–38, 58–61

inpatient treatment, 38, 58–61, 63
insulin, 20

Jackson, Janet, 17
Jamil, Jameela, 51

Kardashian, Kim, 50–51
kidneys, 14, 20, 35

Latinx population, 31
Lovato, Demi, 21

nails, 36, 41
National Association of Anorexia Nervosa and Associated Disorders (ANAD), 10
National Eating Disorders Association (NEDA), 30, 50, 60

Native Americans, 31
Neil, Kimberly, 9, 41
1960s fashion, 26–28
nutritionists, 59, 63

orthorexia, 19–20, 52
outpatient treatment, 58, 60–61, 63

pica, 17
pregnancy, 17
pro-ED content, 68
psychiatrists, 16, 26, 37, 39, 48
psychologists, 21, 28, 39, 40
purging, 9, 14, 15, 23, 28–29, 30–31, 32, 34, 55, 60
    diuretics, 10, 50
    laxatives, 10, 12, 13–14, 31, 34–35, 50, 51, 55
    vomiting, 11, 13–14, 29, 34, 35, 37

raw food diet, 25
rumination syndrome, 17–18, 31

school, 4, 6, 35, 43, 45, 52, 61, 69
SELF magazine, 19, 21
self-care, 69
self-esteem, 14
self-harm, 14–15
side effects, 64–67
Sidibe, Gabourey, 15
skin, 36, 41
sleep apnea, 16
social media, 50, 68
symptoms of eating disorders
    acid reflux, 34
    dizziness, 35

# INDEX
# CONTINUED

gum disease, 14

heart problems, 12–13, 14, 16, 20, 34–35

iron deficiency, 17

isolation, 8, 16, 33, 36, 41, 45, 53

lanugo, 13

malnutrition, 9, 17, 28, 35

menstruation, effects on, 12, 14, 35

sleep problems, 12

tooth decay, 14, 35

weight loss, 6, 12, 18–19, 23, 32, 34, 38, 44, 48–50, 68

*Teen Vogue*, 9, 58

thyroid, 35

transgender population, 30–31

triggers, 16–17, 68–69

Twiggy, 26–28

types of medication

anti-anxiety medications, 39, 64–65

antidepressants, 39, 64–65, 67

antipsychotics, 64, 66

mood stabilizers, 64–65

stimulants, 64, 66–67

types of therapy

art therapy, 63

cognitive behavioral therapy (CBT), 62–63

dance movement therapy, 63

dialectical behavioral therapy (DBT), 63

equine therapy, 63–64

exposure therapy, 64

family therapy, 40, 61

group therapy, 59–61

medical nutrition therapy, 63

weight-class sports, 50

Weiss, Suzannah, 53–54

Winehouse, Amy, 14

work, 16, 35, 43, 51, 61, 69

# IMAGE CREDITS

# ABOUT
# THE AUTHOR

Bethany Bryan has written and edited numerous books for kids and teens. The subject of eating disorders is close to her heart, as a lifelong sufferer of binge-eating disorder, trichotillomania, and dermatillomania linked to anxiety and depression. Luckily, she got help, although she knows she'll never be cured. She urges people in similar situations to seek help, and acknowledges that it can be really, really hard to do, but there are people out there who care. Bryan lives in Kansas City, Missouri.